CAMBRIDGE LIBRARY COLLECTION

Books of enduring scholarly value

Religion

For centuries, scripture and theology were the focus of prodigious amounts of scholarship and publishing, dominated in the English-speaking world by the work of Protestant Christians. Enlightenment philosophy and science, anthropology, ethnology and the colonial experience all brought new perspectives, lively debates and heated controversies to the study of religion and its role in the world, many of which continue to this day. This series explores the editing and interpretation of religious texts, the history of religious ideas and institutions, and not least the encounter between religion and science.

The Destiny of Man

In 1884, American historian and philosopher John Fiske published The Destiny of Man, which discussed humanity's origin, destiny and place in the universe. A leading populariser of Darwin's theory in the United States and influenced by Herbert Spencer, Fiske considers views of human progress via evolutionary social change and the harmony between science and religion. The Destiny of Man is composed of sixteen chapters that anticipate philosophical questions from a typical non-scientific audience: the origins of atheism, the shifting hierarchal positions of humanity through history as proposed by Copernicus and later by Darwin, human brain size, and the 'dawning of consciousness' as a result of the growth and development of moral sentiment and inventiveness through natural selection. Interestingly, at the end of the book, Fiske discusses the historical power relationships of ruling governments and predicts that as humans evolve and become more civilised, war will eventually end.

T0371214

Cambridge University Press has long been a pioneer in the reissuing of out-of-print titles from its own backlist, producing digital reprints of books that are still sought after by scholars and students but could not be reprinted economically using traditional technology. The Cambridge Library Collection extends this activity to a wider range of books which are still of importance to researchers and professionals, either for the source material they contain, or as landmarks in the history of their academic discipline.

Drawing from the world-renowned collections in the Cambridge University Library, and guided by the advice of experts in each subject area, Cambridge University Press is using state-of-the-art scanning machines in its own Printing House to capture the content of each book selected for inclusion. The files are processed to give a consistently clear, crisp image, and the books finished to the high quality standard for which the Press is recognised around the world. The latest print-on-demand technology ensures that the books will remain available indefinitely, and that orders for single or multiple copies can quickly be supplied.

The Cambridge Library Collection will bring back to life books of enduring scholarly value (including out-of-copyright works originally issued by other publishers) across a wide range of disciplines in the humanities and social sciences and in science and technology.

The Destiny of Man

Viewed in the Light of his Origin

JOHN FISKE

CAMBRIDGE UNIVERSITY PRESS

Cambridge, New York, Melbourne, Madrid, Cape Town, Singapore,
São Paolo, Delhi, Dubai, Tokyo

Published in the United States of America by Cambridge University Press, New York

www.cambridge.org
Information on this title: www.cambridge.org/9781108005135

© in this compilation Cambridge University Press 2009

This edition first published 1884
This digitally printed version 2009

ISBN 978-1-108-00513-5 Paperback

THE DESTINY OF MAN
VIEWED IN THE LIGHT
OF HIS ORIGIN

By JOHN FISKE

London
MACMILLAN AND CO.
1884

To

MY CHILDREN,

MAUD, HAROLD, CLARENCE, RALPH,
ETHEL, AND HERBERT,

𝔗𝔥𝔦𝔰 𝔈𝔰𝔰𝔞𝔶

IS LOVINGLY DEDICATED.

PREFACE.

———◆———

AVING been invited to give an address before the Concord School of Philosophy this summer, upon some subject relating to the question of immortality there under discussion, it seemed a proper occasion for putting together the following thoughts on the origin of Man and his place in the universe. In dealing with the unknown, it is well to take one's start a long way within the limits of the known. The question of a future life is generally regarded as lying outside the range of legitimate scientific discussion. Yet while fully admitting this, one does not necessarily admit that the subject is one with regard to which we are forever debarred from entertaining an opinion. Now our opinions on such transcendental questions must necessarily be affected by the total mass of our opinions on the questions which lie within the scope of scientific inquiry ; and from this point of view it becomes of surpassing interest to trace the career of Humanity within that segment of the universe which is accessible to us. The teachings of the doctrine of evolution as to the origin and destiny of Man have, moreover, a very great speculative and practical value of their own, quite apart from their bearings upon any ultimate questions. The body of this essay is accordingly devoted to setting forth these teachings in what I conceive to be their true light ; while their transcendental implications are reserved for the sequel.

As the essay contains an epitome of my own original contributions to the doctrine of evolution, I have added at the end a short list of references to other works of mine, where the points here briefly mentioned are more fully argued and illustrated. The views regarding the progress of human society, and the elimination of warfare, are set forth at greater length in a little book now in the press, and soon to appear, entitled "American Political Ideas."

PETERSHAM, *September* 6, 1884.

CONTENTS.

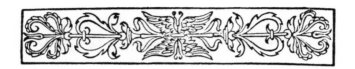

THE DESTINY OF MAN.

I.

Man's Place in Nature, as affected by the Copernican Theory.

WHEN we study the Divine Comedy of Dante — that wonderful book wherein all the knowledge and speculation, all the sorrows and yearnings, of the far-off Middle Ages are enshrined in the glory of imperishable verse — we are brought face to face with a theory of the world and with ways of reasoning about the facts of nature which seem strange to us to-day, but from the influence of which we are not yet, and doubtless never shall be, wholly freed. A cosmology grotesque enough in the light of later knowledge, yet wrought out no less carefully than the

physical theories of Lucretius, is employed
in the service of a theology cumbrous in
its obsolete details, but resting upon fundamental truths which mankind can never
safely lose sight of. In the view of Dante
and of that phase of human culture which
found in him its clearest and sweetest
voice, this earth, the fair home of man,
was placed in the centre of a universe
wherein all things were ordained for his
sole behoof : the sun to give him light and
warmth, the stars in their courses to pre-
side over his strangely checkered destinies,
the winds to blow, the floods to rise, or the
fiend of pestilence to stalk abroad over the
land, — all for the blessing, or the warning,
or the chiding, of the chief among God's
creatures, Man. Upon some such conception as this, indeed, all theology would
seem naturally to rest. Once dethrone
Humanity, regard it as a mere local incident in an endless and aimless series
of cosmical changes, and you arrive at a
doctrine which, under whatever specious

name it may be veiled, is at bottom neither more nor less than Atheism. On its metaphysical side Atheism is the denial of anything psychical in the universe outside of human consciousness ; and it is almost inseparably associated with the materialistic interpretation of human consciousness as the ephemeral result of a fleeting collocation of particles of matter. Viewed upon this side, it is easy to show that Atheism is very bad metaphysics, while the materialism which goes with it is utterly condemned by modern science.[1] But our feeling toward Atheism goes much deeper than the mere recognition of it as philosophically untrue. The mood in which we condemn it is not at all like the mood in which we reject the corpuscular theory of light or Sir G. C. Lewis's vagaries on the subject of Egyptian hieroglyphics. We are wont to look upon Atheism with unspeakable horror and loathing. Our moral sense revolts against it no less than our intelligence ; and this is because, on its practical side, Atheism would remove Humanity from its peculiar position in the world, and make it cast in its lot with the grass that withers and the beasts that perish ; and thus the rich and varied life of the universe, in all the ages of its wondrous duration, becomes deprived of any such element of purpose as can make it intelligible to us or appeal to our moral sympathies and religious aspirations.

And yet the first result of some of the grandest and most irrefragable truths of modern science, when newly discovered and dimly comprehended, has been to make it appear that Humanity must be rudely unseated from its throne in the world and made to occupy an utterly subordinate and trivial position ; and it is because of this mistaken view of their import that the Church has so often and so bitterly opposed the teaching of such truths. With the advent of the Copernican astronomy the funnel-shaped Inferno, the steep mountain of Purgatory crowned

with its terrestrial paradise, and those concentric spheres of Heaven wherein beati-
fied saints held weird and subtle converse,
all went their way to the limbo prepared
for the childlike fancies of untaught minds,
whither Hades and Valhalla had gone before them. In our day it is hard to realize
the startling effect of the discovery that
Man does not dwell at the centre of things,
but is the denizen of an obscure and tiny
speck of cosmical matter quite invisible
amid the innumerable throng of flaming
suns that make up our galaxy. To the
contemporaries of Copernicus the new theory seemed to strike at the very foundations of Christian theology. In a universe
where so much had been made without discernible reference to Man, what became of
that elaborate scheme of salvation which
seemed to rest upon the assumption that
the career of Humanity was the sole object of God's creative forethought and fos-
tering care ? When we bear this in mind,
we see how natural and inevitable it was

that the Church should persecute such
men as Galileo and Bruno. At the same
time it is instructive to observe that, while
the Copernican astronomy has become
firmly established in spite of priestly op-
position, the foundations of Christian theology have not been shaken thereby. It
is not that the question which once so
sorely puzzled men has ever been settled,
but that it has been outgrown. The speculative necessity for man's occupying the
largest and most central spot in the universe is no longer felt. It is recognized as
a primitive and childish notion. With our
larger knowledge we see that these vast
and fiery suns are after all but the Titan-
like *servants* of the little planets which
they bear with them in their flight through
the abysses of space. Out from the awful
gaseous turmoil of the central mass dart
those ceaseless waves of gentle radiance
that, when caught upon the surface of
whirling worlds like ours, bring forth the
endlessly varied forms and the endlessly

complex movements that make up what we can see of life. And as when God revealed himself to his ancient prophet He came not in the earthquake or the tempest but in a voice that was still and small, so that divine spark the Soul, as it takes up its brief abode in this realm of fleeting phenomena, chooses not the central sun where elemental forces forever blaze and clash, but selects an outlying terrestrial nook where seeds may germinate in silence, and where through slow fruition the mysterious forms of organic life may come to take shape and thrive. He who thus looks a little deeper into the secrets of nature than his forefathers of the sixteenth century may well smile at the quaint conceit that man cannot be the object of God's care unless he occupies an immovable position in the centre of the stellar universe.

2

II.

Man's Place in Nature, as affected by Darwinism.

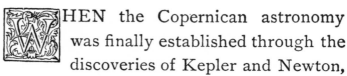HEN the Copernican astronomy was finally established through the discoveries of Kepler and Newton, it might well have been pronounced the greatest scientific achievement of the human mind ; but it was still more than that. It was the greatest revolution that had ever been effected in Man's views of his relations to the universe in which he lives, and of which he is — at least during the present life — a part. During the nineteenth century, however, a still greater revolution has been effected. Not only has Lyell enlarged our mental horizon in time as much as Newton enlarged it in space, but it appears that throughout these vast stretches of time and space with which

we have been made acquainted there are sundry well-marked changes going on. Certain definite paths of development are being pursued ; and around us on every side we behold worlds, organisms, and societies in divers stages of progress or decline. Still more, as we examine the records of past life upon our globe, and study the mutual relations of the living things that still remain, it appears that the higher forms of life — including Man himself — are the modified descendants of lower forms. Zoölogically speaking, Man can no longer be regarded as a creature apart by himself. We cannot erect an order on purpose to contain him, as Cuvier tried to do ; we cannot even make a separate family for him. Man is not only a vertebrate, a mammal, and a primate, but he belongs, as a genus, to the catarrhine family of apes. And just as lions, leopards, and lynxes — different genera of the cat-family — are descended from a common stock of carnivora, back to

which we may also trace the pedigrees of
dogs, hyænas, bears, and seals ; so the various genera of platyrrhine and catarrhine
apes, including Man, are doubtless descended from a common stock of primates,
back to which we may also trace the con-
verging pedigrees of monkeys and lemurs,
until their ancestry becomes indistinguish-
able from that of rabbits and squirrels.
Such is the conclusion to which the scientific world has come within a quarter of a
century from the publication of Mr. Darwin's "Origin of Species;" and there is
no more reason for supposing that this
conclusion will ever be gainsaid than for
supposing that the Copernican astronomy
will some time be overthrown and the
concentric spheres of Dante's heaven re-
instated in the minds of men.

It is not strange that this theory of
man's origin, which we associate mainly
with the name of Mr. Darwin, should be
to many people very unwelcome. It is
fast bringing about a still greater revolu-

tion in thought than that which was heralded by Copernicus ; and it naturally takes
some time for the various portions of one's
theory of things to become adjusted, one
after another, to so vast and sweeping a
change. From many quarters the cry goes
up, — If this be true, then Man is at length
cast down from his high position in the
world. "I will not be called a mammal,
or the son of a mammal!" once exclaimed
an acquaintance of mine who perhaps had
been brought up by hand. Such expres-
sions of feeling are crude, but the feeling is
not unjustifiable. It is urged that if man
is physically akin to a baboon, as pigs are
akin to horses, and cows to deer, then Humanity can in nowise be regarded as occupying a peculiar place in the universe ; it
becomes a mere incident in an endless series of changes, and how can we say that
the same process of evolution that has produced mankind may not by and by produce
something far more perfect ? There was a
time when huge bird-like reptiles were the

lords of creation, and after these had been
" sealed within the iron hills " there came
successive dynasties of mammals ; and as
the iguanodon gave place to the great Eo-
cene marsupials, as the mastodon and the
sabre-toothed lion have long since van-
ished from the scene, so may not Man by
and by disappear to make way for some
higher creature, and so on forever ? In
such case, why should we regard Man as
in any higher sense the object of Divine
care than a pig? Still stronger does the
case appear when we remember that those
countless adaptations of means to ends in
nature, which since the time of Voltaire
and Paley we have been accustomed to
cite as evidences of creative design, have
received at the hands of Mr. Darwin a
very different interpretation. The lob-
ster's powerful claw, the butterfly's gor-
geous tints, the rose's delicious fragrance,
the architectural instinct of the bee, the
astonishing structure of the orchid, are no
longer explained as the results of contri-

vance. That simple but wasteful process of survival of the fittest, through which such marvellous things have come into being, has little about it that is analogous to the ingenuity of human art. The infinite and eternal Power which is thus revealed in the physical life of the universe seems in nowise akin to the human soul. The idea of beneficent purpose seems for the moment to be excluded from nature, and a blind process, known as Natural Selection, is the deity that slumbers not nor sleeps. Reckless of good and evil, it brings forth at once the mother's tender love for her infant and the horrible teeth of the ravening shark, and to its creative indifference the one is as good as the other.

In spite of these appalling arguments the man of science, urged by the single-hearted purpose to ascertain the truth, be the consequences what they may, goes quietly on and finds that the terrible theory must be adopted; the fact of man's consanguinity with dumb beasts must be admitted. In

reaching this conclusion, the man of science reasons upon the physical facts within
his reach, applying to them the same principles of common-sense whereby our every-
day lives are successfully guided ; and he is
very apt to smile at the methods of those
people who, taking hold of the question at
the wrong end, begin by arguing about all
manner of fancied consequences. For his
knowledge of the history of human thinking assures him that such methods have
through all past time proved barren of
aught save strife, while his own bold yet
humble method is the only one through
which truth has ever been elicited. To
pursue unflinchingly the methods of science requires dauntless courage and a faith
that nothing can shake. Such courage
and such loyalty to nature brings its own
reward. For when once the formidable
theory is really understood, when once its
implications are properly unfolded, it is
seen to have no such logical consequences
as were at first ascribed to it. As with

the Copernican astronomy, so with the Darwinian biology, we rise to a higher view of the workings of God and of the nature of Man than was ever attainable before. So far from degrading Humanity, or putting it on a level with the animal world in general, the Darwinian theory shows us distinctly for the first time how the creation and the perfecting of Man is the goal toward which Nature's work has all the while been tending. It enlarges tenfold the significance of human life, places it upon even a loftier eminence than poets or prophets have imagined, and makes it seem more than ever the chief object of that creative activity which is manifested in the physical universe.

III.

On the Earth there will never be a Higher Creature than Man.

IN elucidating these points, we may fitly begin by considering the question as to the possibility of the evolution of any higher creature than Man, to whom the dominion over this earth shall pass. The question will best be answered by turning back and observing one of the most remarkable features connected with the origin of Man and with his superiority over other animals. And let it be borne in mind that we are not now about to wander through the regions of unconditional possibility. We are not dealing with vague general notions of development, but with the scientific Darwinian theory, which alleges development only as the result of certain rigorously defined agencies. The chief among these agencies is Natural Selection. It has again and again been illustrated how by the cumulative selection and inheritance of slight physical variations generic differences, like those between the tiger and the leopard, or the cow and the antelope, at length arise; and the guiding principle in the accumulation of slight physical differences has been the welfare of the species. The variant forms on either side have survived while the constant forms have perished, so that the lines of demarcation between allied species have grown more and more distinct, and it is usually only by going back to fossil ages that we can supply the missing links of continuity. In the desperate struggle for existence no peculiarity, physical or psychical, however slight, has been too insignificant for natural selection to seize and enhance; and the myriad fantastic forms and hues of animal and vegetal life illustrate the seeming capriciousness of its workings. Psychical variations have never been unimportant

since the appearance of the first faint pigment-spot which by and by was to translate
touch into vision, as it developed into the
lenses and humours of the eye.[2] Special
organs of sense and the lower grades of
perception and judgment were slowly developed through countless ages, in com-
pany with purely physical variations of
shape of foot, or length of neck, or complexity of stomach, or thickness of hide.
At length there came a wonderful moment
— silent and unnoticed, as are the beginnings of all great revolutions. Silent and
unnoticed, even as the day of the Lord
which cometh like a thief in the night,
there arrived that wonderful moment at
which psychical changes began to be of
more use than physical changes to the
brute ancestor of Man. Through further
ages of ceaseless struggle the profitable
variations in this creature occurred oftener
and oftener in the brain, and less often in
other parts of the organism, until by and
by the size of his brain had been doubled

and its complexity of structure increased a thousand-fold, while in other respects his appearance was not so very different from that of his brother apes.[3] Along with this growth of the brain, the complete assumption of the upright posture, enabling the hands to be devoted entirely to prehension and thus relieving the jaws of that part of their work, has coöperated in producing that peculiar contour of head and face which is the chief distinguishing mark of physical Man. These slight anatomical changes derive their importance entirely from the prodigious intellectual changes in connection with which they have been produced ; and these intellectual changes have been accumulated until the distance, psychically speaking, between civilized man and the ape is so great as to dwarf in comparison all that had been achieved in the process of evolution down to the time of our half-human ancestor's first appearance. No fact in nature is fraught with deeper meaning than this two-sided fact of the

extreme physical similarity and enormous
psychical divergence between Man and the
group of animals to which he traces his
pedigree.   It shows that when Humanity began to be evolved an entirely new
chapter in the history of the universe was
opened.   Henceforth the life of the nas-
cent soul came to be first in importance,
and the bodily life became subordinated to
it.   Henceforth it appeared that, in this
direction at least, the process of zoölogical
change had come to an end, and a process
of psychological change was to take its
place.   Henceforth along this supreme line
of generation there was to be no further
evolution of new species through physical
variation, but through the accumulation of
psychical variations one particular species
was to be indefinitely perfected and raised
to a totally different plane from that on
which all life had hitherto existed.   Henceforth, in short, the dominant aspect of evolution was to be not the genesis of species, but the progress of Civilization.

As we thoroughly grasp the meaning of all this, we see that upon the Darwinian theory it is impossible that any creature zoölogically distinct from Man and superior to him should ever at any future time exist upon the earth. In the regions of unconditional possibility it is open to any one to argue, if he chooses, that such a creature may come to exist ; but the Darwinian theory is utterly opposed to any such conclusion. According to Darwinism, the creation of Man is still the goal toward which Nature tended from the beginning. Not the production of any higher creature, but the perfecting of Humanity, is to be the glorious consummation of Nature's long and tedious work. Thus we suddenly arrive at the conclusion that Man seems now, much more clearly than ever, the chief among God's creatures. On the primitive barbaric theory, which Mr. Darwin has swept away, Man was suddenly flung into the world by the miraculous act of some unseen and incalculable Power act-ing from without ; and whatever theology might suppose, no scientific reason could be alleged why the same incalculable Power might not at some future moment, by a similar miracle, thrust upon the scene some mightier creature in whose presence Man would become like a sorry beast of burden. But he who has mastered the Darwinian theory, he who recognizes the slow and subtle process of evolution as the way in which God makes things come to pass, must take a far higher view. He sees that in the deadly struggle for existence which has raged throughout countless æons of time, the whole creation has been groaning and travailing together in order to bring forth that last consummate speci- men of God's handiwork, the Human Soul.

To the creature thus produced through a change in the direction in which natural selection has worked, the earth and most of its living things have become gradually subordinated. In all the classes of the animal and vegetal worlds many ancient

species have become extinct, and many
modern species have come into being,
through the unchecked working of natural
selection, since Man became distinctively
human. But in this respect a change has
long been coming over the face of nature.
The destinies of all other living things are
more and more dependent upon the will of
Man. It rests with him to determine, to a
great degree, what plants and animals shall
remain upon the earth and what shall be
swept from its surface. By unconsciously
imitating the selective processes of Nature, he long ago wrought many wild species into forms subservient to his needs.
He has created new varieties of fruit and
flower and cereal grass, and has reared
new breeds of animals to aid him in the
work of civilization ; until at length he is
beginning to acquire a mastery over me-
chanical and molecular and chemical forces
which is doubtless destined in the future
to achieve marvellous results whereof to-
day we little dream. Natural selection

3

itself will by and by occupy a subordinate place in comparison with selection by Man, whose appearance on the earth is thus seen more clearly than ever to have opened an entirely new chapter in the mysterious history of creation.

IV.

The Origin of Infancy.

BUT before we can fully understand the exalted position which the Darwinian theory assigns to man, another point demands consideration. The natural selection of psychical peculiarities does not alone account for the origin of Man, or explain his most signal difference from all other animals. That difference is unquestionably a difference in kind, but in saying this one must guard against misunderstanding. Not only in the world of organic life, but throughout the known universe, the doctrine of evolution regards differences in kind as due to the gradual accumulation of differences in degree. To cite a very simple case, what differences of kind can be more striking than the differences between a nebula, a sun, a planet

like the earth, and a planet like our moon ?
Yet these things are simply examples of
cosmical matter at four different stages of
cooling.   The physical differences between
steam, water, and ice afford a more familiar example.   In the organic world the perpetual modification of structures that has
been effected through natural selection ex-
hibits countless instances of differences in
kind which have risen from the accumulation of differences in degree.   No one
would hesitate to call a horse's hoof different in kind from a cat's paw ; yet a hoof
is made up of five claws grown together
and furnished with a nail in common.   The
most signal differences in kind are wont to
arise when organs originally developed for
a certain purpose come to be applied to a
very different purpose, as that change of
the fish's air-bladder into a lung which accompanied the first development of land
vertebrates.   But still greater becomes the
revolution when a certain process goes on
until it sets going a number of other proc-

esses, unlocking series after series of causal agencies until a vast and complicated result is reached, such as could by no possibility have been foreseen. The creation of Man was one of these vast and complicated results due to the unlocking of various series of causal agencies ; and it was the beginning of a deeper and mightier difference in kind than any that slowly-evolving Nature had yet witnessed.

I have indicated, as the moment at which the creation of mankind began, the moment when psychical variations became of so much more use to our ancestors than physical variations that they were seized and enhanced by natural selection, to the comparative neglect of the latter. Increase of intellectual capacity, in connection with the developing brain of a single race of creatures, now became the chief work of natural selection in originating Man ; and this, I say, was the opening of a new chapter, the last and most wonderful chapter, in the history of creation. But the increasing intelligence and enlarged experience of half-human man now set in motion a new series of changes which greatly complicated the matter. In order to understand these changes, we must consider for a moment one very important characteristic of developing intelligence.

The simplest actions in which the nervous system is concerned are what we call reflex actions. All the visceral actions which keep us alive from moment to moment, the movements of the heart and lungs, the contractions of arteries, the secretions of glands, the digestive operations of the stomach and liver, belong to the class of reflex actions. Throughout the animal world these acts are repeated, with little or no variation, from birth until death, and the tendency to perform them is completely organized in the nervous system before birth. Every animal breathes and digests as well at the beginning of his life as he ever does. Contact with air and food is all that is needed, and there is nothing to be learned. These actions, though they are performed by the nervous system, we do not class as psychical, because they are nearly or quite unattended by consciousness. The psychical life of the lowest animals consists of a few simple acts directed toward the securing of food and the avoidance of danger, and these acts we are in the habit of classing as instinctive. They are so simple, so few, and so often repeated, that the tendency to perform them is completely organized in the nervous system before birth. The animal takes care of himself as soon as he begins to live. He has nothing to learn, and his career is a simple repetition of the careers of countless ancestors. With him heredity is everything, and his individual experience is next to nothing.

As we ascend the animal scale till we come to the higher birds and mammals, we find a very interesting and remarkable change beginning. The general increase of intelligence involves an increasing variety and complication of experiences. The acts which the animal performs in the course of its life become far more numerous, far more various, and far more complex. They are therefore severally repeated with less frequency in the lifetime of each individual. Consequently the tendency to perform them is not completely organized in the nervous system of the offspring before birth. The short period of ante-natal existence does not afford time enough for the organization of so many and such complex habitudes and capacities. The process which in the lower animals is completed before birth is in the higher animals left to be completed after birth. When the creature begins its life it is not completely organized. Instead of the power of doing all the things which its parents did, it starts with the power of doing only some few of them; for the rest it has only latent capacities which need to be brought out by its individual experience after birth. In other words, it begins its separate life not as a matured creature, but as an infant which needs for a time to be watched and helped.

V.

The Dawning of Consciousness.

ERE we arrive at one of the most wonderful moments in the history of creation, — the moment of the first faint dawning of consciousness, the foreshadowing of the true life of the soul. Whence came the soul we no more know than we know whence came the universe. The primal origin of consciousness is hidden in the depths of the bygone eternity. That it cannot possibly be the product of any cunning arrangement of material particles is demonstrated beyond peradventure by what we now know of the correlation of physical forces.[4] The Platonic view of the soul, as a spiritual substance, an effluence from Godhood, which under certain conditions becomes incarnated in perishable forms of matter, is doubtless the view most consonant with the present state of our knowledge. Yet while we know not the primal origin of the soul, we have learned something with regard to the conditions under which it has become incarnated in material forms. Modern psychology has something to say about the dawning of conscious life in the animal world. Reflex action is unaccompanied by consciousness. The nervous actions which regulate the movements of the viscera go on without our knowledge ; we learn of their existence only by study, as we learn of facts in outward nature. If you tickle the foot of a person asleep, and the foot is withdrawn by simple reflex action, the sleeper is unconscious alike of the irritation and of the movement, even as the decapitated frog is unconscious when a drop of nitric acid falls on his back and he lifts up a leg and rubs the place. In like manner the reflex movements which make up the life of the lowest animals are doubtless quite unconscious, even when in their general character they simulate conscious actions, as they often do. In the case of such creatures, the famous hypothesis of Descartes, that animals are automata, is doubtless mainly correct. In the case of instincts also, where the instinctive actions are completely organized before birth, and are repeated without variation during the whole lifetime of the individual, there is probably little if any consciousness. It is an essential prerequisite of consciousness that there should be a period of delay or tension between the receipt of an impression and the determination of the consequent movement. Diminish this period of delay and you diminish the vividness of consciousness. A familiar example will make this clear. When you are learning to play a new piece of music on the piano, especially if you do not read music rapidly, you are intensely conscious of each group of notes on the page, and of each group of keys that you strike, and of the relations of the one to the other. But when you have learned the piece by heart, you think nothing of either notes or keys, but play automatically while your attention is concentrated upon the artistic character of the music. If somebody thoughtlessly interrupts you with a question about Egyptian politics, you go on playing while you answer him politely. That is, where you had at first to make a conscious act of volition for each movement, the whole group of movements has now become automatic, and volition is only concerned in setting the process going. As the delay involved in the perception and the movement disappears, so does the consciousness of the perception and the movement tend to disappear. Consciousness implies perpetual discrimination, or the recognition of likenesses and differences, and this is impossible unless impressions persist long enough to be compared with one another. The physical organs in connection with whose activity consciousness is manifested are the upper and outer parts of the brain, — the

cerebrum and cerebellum. These organs
never receive impressions directly from
the outside world, but only from lower
nerve-centres, such as the spinal cord, the
medulla, the optic lobes, and other special·
centres of sensation. The impressions received by the cerebrum and cerebellum
are waves of molecular disturbance sent
up along centripetal nerves from the lower
centres, and presently drafted off along
centrifugal nerves back to the lower centres, thus causing the myriad movements
which make up our active life. Now there
is no consciousness except when molecular disturbance is generated in the cerebrum and cerebellum faster than it can be
drafted off to the lower centres.[5] It is the
surplus of molecular disturbance remain-
ing in the cerebrum and cerebellum, and
reflected back and forth among the cells
and fibres of which these highest centres
are composed, that affords the physical
condition for the manifestation of consciousness. Memory, emotion, reason, and

volition begin with this retention of a surplus of molecular motion in the highest centres. As we survey the vertebrate
sub-kingdom of animals, we find that as
this surplus increases, the surface of the
highest centres increases in area. In the
lowest vertebrate animal, the amphioxus,
the cerebrum and cerebellum do not exist
at all. In fishes we begin to find them,
but they are much smaller than the optic
lobes. In such a highly organized fish as
the halibut, which weighs about as much
as an average-sized man, the cerebrum is
smaller than a melon-seed. Continuing
to grow by adding concentric layers at
the surface, the cerebrum and cerebellum
become much larger in birds and lower
mammals, gradually covering up the optic
lobes. As we pass to higher mammalian
forms, the growth of the cerebrum becomes most conspicuous, until it extends
backwards so far as to cover up the cerebellum, whose functions are limited to the
conscious adjustment of muscular move-

ments. In the higher apes the cerebrum begins to extend itself forwards, and this goes on in the human race. The cranial capacity of the European exceeds that of the Australian by forty cubic inches, or nearly four times as much as that by which the Australian exceeds the gorilla ; and the expansion is almost entirely in the upper and anterior portions. But the increase of the cerebral surface is shown not only in the general size of the organ, but to a still greater extent in the irregular creasing and furrowing of the surface. This creasing and furrowing begins to occur in the higher mammals, and in civilized man it is carried to an astonishing extent. The amount of intelligence is correlated with the number, the depth, and the irregularity of the furrows. A cat's brain has a few symmetrical creases. In an ape the creases are deepened into slight furrows, and they run irregularly, somewhat like the lines in the palm of your hand. With age and experience the furrows grow deeper and more sinuous, and new ones appear ; and in man these phenomena come to have great significance. The cerebral surface of a human infant is like that of an ape. In an adult savage, or in a European peasant, the furrowing is somewhat marked and complicated. In the brain of a great scholar, the furrows are very deep and crooked, and hundreds of creases appear which are not found at all in the brains of ordinary men. In other words, the cerebral surface of such a man, the seat of conscious mental life, has become enormously enlarged in area ; and we must further observe that it goes on enlarging in some cases into extreme old age.[6]

Putting all these facts together, it becomes plain that in the lowest animals, whose lives consist of sundry reflex actions monotonously repeated from generation to generation, there can be nothing, or next to nothing, of what we know as consciousness. It is only when the life becomes more complicated and various, so that reflex action can no longer determine all its movements and the higher nerve-centres begin to be evolved, that the dawning of consciousness is reached. But with the growth of the higher centres the capacities of action become so various and indeterminate that definite direction is not given to them until after birth. The creature begins life as an infant, with its partially developed cerebrum representing capabilities which it is left for its individual experience to bring forth and modify.

VI.

Lengthening of Infancy, and Concomitant Increase of Brain-Surface.

THE first appearance of infancy in the animal world thus heralded the new era which was to be crowned by the development of Man. With the beginnings of infancy there came the first dawning of a conscious life similar in nature to the conscious life of human beings, and there came, moreover, on the part of parents, the beginning of feelings and actions not purely self-regarding. But still more, the period of infancy was a period of plasticity. The career of each individual being no longer wholly pre-determined by the careers of its ancestors, it began to become teachable. Individuality of character also became possible at the same time, and for the same reason.

All birds and mammals which take care of their young are teachable, though in very various degrees, and all in like manner show individual peculiarities of disposition, though in most cases these are slight and inconspicuous. In dogs, horses, and apes there is marked teachableness, and there are also marked differences in individual character.

But in the non-human animal world all these phenomena are but slightly developed. They are but the dim adumbrations of what was by and by to bloom forth in the human race. They can scarcely be said to have served as a prophecy of the revolution that was to come. One generation of dumb beasts is after all very like another, and from studying the careers of the mastodon, the hipparion, the sabre-toothed lion, or even the dryopithecus, an observer in the Miocene age could never have foreseen the possibility of a creature endowed with such a boundless capacity of progress as the modern Man. Nevertheless, however dimly suggestive was this group of phenomena, it contained the germ of all that is preëminent in humanity. In the direct line of our ancestry it only needed that the period of infancy should be sufficiently prolonged, in order that a creature should at length appear, endowed with the teachableness, the individuality, and the capacity for progress which are the peculiar prerogatives of fully-developed Man.[7]   In this direct line the manlike apes of Africa and the Indian Archipelago have advanced far beyond the mammalian world in general. Along with a cerebral surface, and an accompanying intelligence, far greater than that of other mammals, these tailless apes begin life as helpless babies, and are unable to walk, to feed themselves, or to grasp objects with precision until they are two or three months old.   These apes have thus advanced a little way upon the peculiar road which our half-human forefathers began to travel as soon as psychical variations came to be of more use to the species than variations in bodily structure. The gulf by which the lowest known man is separated from the highest known ape consists in the great increase of his cerebral surface, with the accompanying intelligence, and in the very long duration of his infancy. These two things have gone hand in hand. The increase of cerebral surface, due to the working of natural selection in this direction alone, has entailed a vast increase in the amount of cerebral organization that must be left to be completed after birth, and thus has prolonged the period of infancy. And conversely the prolonging of the plastic period of infancy, entailing a vast increase in teachableness and versatility, has contributed to the further enlargement of the cerebral surface. The mutual reaction of these two groups of facts must have gone on for an enormous length of time since man began thus diverging from his simian brethren. It is not likely that less than a

million years have elapsed since the first
page of this new chapter in the history of
creation was opened : it is probable that
the time has been much longer. In comparison with such a period, the whole re-
corded duration of human history shrinks
into nothingness. The pyramids of Egypt
seem like things of yesterday when we
think of the Cave-Men of western Europe
in the glacial period, who scratched pic-
tures of mammoths on pieces of reindeer-
antler with a bit of pointed flint. Yet
during an entire geologic æon before these
Cave-Men appeared on the scene, "a being
erect upon two legs," if we may quote
from Serjeant Buzfuz, "and wearing the
outward semblance of a man and not of a
monster," wandered hither and thither
over the face of the earth, setting his
mark upon it as no other creature yet had
done, leaving behind him innumerable
tell-tale remnants of his fierce and squalid
existence, yet too scantily endowed with
wit to make any written disclosure of his

thoughts and deeds.   If the physiological
annals of that long and weary time could
now be unrolled before us, the principal
fact which we should discern, dominating
all other facts in interest and significance,
would be that mutual reaction between increase of cerebral surface and lengthening
of babyhood which I have here described.

Thus through the simple continuance
and interaction of processes that began far
back in the world of warm-blooded animals,
we get at last a creature essentially different from all others.   Through the complication of effects the heaping up of minute
differences in degree has ended in bringing forth a difference in kind.   In the human organism physical variation has well-
nigh stopped, or is confined to insignificant
features, save in the grey surface of the
cerebrum.   The work of cerebral organization is chiefly completed after birth, as
we see by contrasting the smooth ape-like
brain-surface of the new-born child with
the   deeply-furrowed   and   myriad-seamed

surface of the adult civilized brain. The plastic period of adolescence, lengthened in civilized man until it has come to cover more than one third of his lifetime, is thus the guaranty of his boundless progressiveness. Inherited tendencies and aptitudes still form the foundations of character ; but individual experience has come to count as an enormous factor in modifying the career of mankind from generation to generation. It is not too much to say that the difference between man and all other living creatures, in respect of teachableness, progressiveness, and individuality of character, surpasses all other differences of kind that are known to exist in the universe.

VII.

Change in the Direction of the Working of Natural Selection.

N the fresh light which these considerations throw upon the problem of man's origin, we can now
see more clearly than ever how great a
revolution was inaugurated when natural
selection began to confine its operations
to the surface of the cerebrum. Among
the older incidents in the evolution of organic life, the changes were very wonderful which out of the pectoral fin of a fish
developed the jointed fore-limb of the
mammal with its five-toed paw, and thence
through much slighter variation brought
forth the human arm with its delicate and
crafty hand. More wondrous still were
the phases of change through which the
rudimentary pigment-spot of the worm, by

the development and differentiation of successive layers, gave place to the variously-constructed eyes of insects, mollusks, and vertebrates. The day for creative work of this sort has probably gone by, as the day for the evolution of annulose segments and vertebrate skeletons has gone by, — on our planet, at least. In the line of our own development, all work of this kind stopped long ago, to be replaced by different methods. As an optical instrument, the eye had well-nigh reached extreme perfection in many a bird and mammal ages before man's beginnings; and the essential features of the human hand existed already in the hands of Miocene apes. But different methods came in when human intelligence appeared upon the scene. Mr. Spencer has somewhere reminded us that the crowbar is but an extra lever added to the levers of which the arm is already composed, and the telescope but adds a new set of lenses to those which already exist in the eye. This beautiful illustration goes to

the kernel of the change that was wrought
when natural selection began to confine itself to the psychical modification of our ancestors.   In a very deep sense all human
science is but the increment of the power
of the eye, and all human art is the increment of the power of the hand.[8]   Vision
and manipulation, — these, in their countless indirect and transfigured forms, are
the two coöperating factors in all intellectual progress.   It is not merely that with
the telescope we see extinct volcanoes on
the moon, or resolve spots of nebulous
cloud into clusters of blazing suns ; it is
that in every scientific theory we frame by
indirect methods visual images of things
not present to sense.   With our mind's
eye we see atmospheric convulsions on the
surfaces of distant worlds, watch the giant
ichthyosaurs splashing in Jurassic oceans,
follow the varied figures of the rhythmic
dance of molecules as chemical elements
unite and separate, or examine, with the
aid of long-forgotten vocabularies now

magically restored, the manners and morals, the laws and superstitions, of peoples that have ceased to be.[9] And so in art the wonderful printing-press, and the engine that moves it, are the lineal descendants through countless stages of complication, of the simple levers of primitive man and the rude stylus wherewith he engraved strange hieroglyphs on the bark of trees. In such ways, since the human phase of evolution began, has the direct action of muscle and sense been supplemented and superseded by the indirect work of the inquisitive and inventive mind.

VIII.

Growing Predominance of the Psychical Life.

LET us note one further aspect of this mighty revolution. In its lowly beginnings the psychical life was merely an appendage to the life of the body. The avoidance of enemies, the securing of food, the perpetuation of the species, make up the whole of the lives of lower animals, and the rudiments of memory, reason, emotion, and volition were at first concerned solely with the achievement of these ends in an increasingly indirect, complex, and effective way. Though the life of a large portion of the human race is still confined to the pursuit of these same ends, yet so vast has been the increase of psychical life that the simple character of the ends is liable to be lost sight of amid the variety, the indirect-ness, and the complexity of the means. But in civilized society other ends, purely immaterial in their nature, have come to add themselves to these, and in some instances to take their place. It is long since we were told that Man does not live by bread alone. During many generations we have seen thousands of men, actuated by the noblest impulse of which humanity is capable, though misled by the teachings of a crude philosophy, despising and maltreating their bodies as clogs and incumbrances to the life of the indwelling soul. Countless martyrs we have seen throwing away the physical earthly life as so much worthless dross, and all for the sake of purely spiritual truths. As with religion, so with the scientific spirit and the artistic spirit, — the unquenchable craving to know the secrets of nature, and the yearning to create the beautiful in form and colour and sound. In the highest human beings such ends as these have come to be uppermost in consciousness, and with the progress of material civilization this will be more and more the case. If we can imagine a future time when warfare and crime shall have been done away with forever, when disease shall have been for the most part curbed, and when every human being by moderate labour can secure ample food and shelter, we can also see that in such a state of things the work of civilization would be by no means completed. In ministering to human happiness in countless ways, through the pursuit of purely spiritual ends, in enriching and diversifying life to the utmost, there would still be almost limitless work to be done. I believe that such a time will come for weary and suffering mankind. Such a faith is inspiring. It sustains one in the work of life, when one would otherwise lose heart. But it is a faith that rests upon induction. The process of evolution is excessively slow, and its ends are achieved at the cost of enormous waste of life, but for innumerable ages its direction has been toward the goal here pointed out ; and the case may be fitly summed up in the statement that whereas in its rude beginnings the psychical life was but an appendage to the body, in fully-developed Humanity the body is but the vehicle for the soul.

IX.

The Origins of Society and of Morality.

ONE further point must be considered before this outline sketch of the manner of man's origin can be called complete. The psychical development of Humanity, since its earlier stages, has been largely due to the reaction of individuals upon one another in those various relations which we characterize as social.[10] In considering the origin of Man, the origin of human society cannot be passed over. Foreshadowings of social relations occur in the animal world, not only in the line of our own vertebrate ancestry, but in certain orders of insects which stand quite remote from that line. Many of the higher mammals are gregarious, and this is especially true of that whole order of primates to which

we belong. Rudimentary moral senti-
ments are also clearly discernible in the
highest members of various mammalian
orders, and in all but the lowest members
of our own order. But in respect of defi-
niteness and permanence the relations between individuals in a state of gregarious-
ness fall far short of the relations between
individuals in the rudest human society.
The primordial unit of human society is
the family, and it was by the establish-
ment of definite and permanent family
relationships that the step was taken
which raised Man socially above the level
of gregarious apehood. This great point
was attained through that lengthening of
the period of helpless childhood which
accompanied the gradually increasing intelligence of our half-human ancestors.
When childhood had come to extend over
a period of ten or a dozen years—a period
which would be doubled, or more than
doubled, where several children were born
in succession to the same parents — the

relationships between father and mother, brethren and sisters, must have become firmly knit ; and thus the family, the unit of human society, gradually came into existence.[11] The rudimentary growth of moral sentiment must now have received a definite direction. As already observed, with the beginnings of infancy in the animal world there came the genesis in the parents of feelings and actions not purely self-regarding. Rudimentary sympathies, with rudimentary capacity for self-devotion, are witnessed now and then among higher mammals, such as the dog, and not uncommonly among apes. But as the human family, with its definite relationships, came into being, there must necessarily have grown up between its various members reciprocal necessities of behaviour. The conduct of the individual could no longer be shaped with sole reference to his own selfish desires, but must be to a great extent subordinated to the general welfare of the family. And in judging of the character of his own conduct, the individual must now begin to refer it to some law of things outside of himself; and hence the germs of conscience and of the idea of duty. Such were no doubt the crude beginnings of human morality.

With this genesis of the family, the Creation of Man may be said, in a certain sense, to have been completed. The great extent of cerebral surface, the lengthened period of infancy, the consequent capacity for progress, the definite constitution of the family, and the judgment of actions as good or bad according to some other standard than that of selfish desire, — these are the attributes which essentially distinguish Man from other creatures. All these, we see, are direct or indirect results of the revolution which began when natural selection came to confine itself to psychical variations, to the neglect of physical variations. The immediate result was the increase of cerebrum. This prolonged the infancy, thus giving rise to the capacity for progress; and infancy, in turn, originated the family and thus opened the way for the growth of sympathies and of ethical feelings.   All these results have perpetually reacted upon one another until a creature different in kind from all other creatures has been evolved.   The creature thus evolved long since became dominant over the earth in a sense in which none of his predecessors ever became dominant; and henceforth the work of evolution, so far as our planet is concerned, is chiefly devoted to the perfecting of this last and most wonderful product of creative energy.

X.

Improvableness of Man.

OR the creation of Man was by no means the creation of a perfect being. The most essential feature of Man is his improvableness, and since his first appearance on the earth the changes that have gone on in him have been enormous, though they have continued to run along in the lines of development that were then marked out. The changes have been so great that in many respects the interval between the highest and the lowest men far surpasses quantitatively the interval between the lowest men and the highest apes. If we take into account the creasing of the cerebral surface, the difference between the brain of a Shakespeare and that of an Australian savage would doubtless be fifty times greater than the difference between the Australian's brain and that of an orang-outang. In mathematical capacity the Australian, who cannot tell the number of fingers on his two hands, is much nearer to a lion or wolf than to Sir Rowan Hamilton, who invented the method of quaternions. In moral development this same Australian, whose language contains no words for justice and benevolence, is less remote from dogs and baboons than from a Howard or a Garrison. In progressiveness, too, the difference between the lowest and the highest races of men is no less conspicuous. The Australian is more teachable than the ape, but his limit is nevertheless very quickly reached. All the distinctive attributes of Man, in short, have been developed to an enormous extent through long ages of social evolution.

This psychical development of Man is destined to go on in the future as it has gone on in the past. The creative energy which has been at work through the bygone

eternity is not going to become quiescent
to-morrow. We have learned something of
its methods of working, and from the care-
ful observation of the past we can foresee
the future in some of its most general outlines. From what has already gone on during the historic period of man's existence,
we can safely predict a change that will
by and by distinguish him from all other
creatures even more widely and more fun-
damentally than he is distinguished to-
day. Whenever in the course of organic
evolution we see any function beginning
as incidental to the performance of other
functions, and continuing for many ages to
increase in importance until it becomes an
indispensable strand in the web of life, we
may be sure that by a continuance of the
same process its influence is destined to
increase still more in the future. Such has
been the case with the function of sympathy, and with the ethical feelings which
have grown up along with sympathy and
depend largely upon it for their vitality.

Like everything else which especially distinguishes Man, the altruistic feelings were first called into existence through the first beginnings of infancy in the animal world. Their rudimentary form was that of the transient affection of a female bird or mammal for its young. First given a definite direction through the genesis of the primitive human-family, the development of altruism has formed an important part of the progress of civilization, but as yet it has scarcely kept pace with the general development of intelligence. There can be little doubt that in respect of justice and kindness the advance of civilized man has been less marked than in respect of quick-wittedness. Now this is because the advancement of civilized man has been largely effected through fighting, through the continuance of that deadly struggle and competition which has been going on ever since organic life first appeared on the earth. It is through such fierce and perpetual struggle that the higher forms of life have been gradually evolved by natural selection. But we have already seen how in many respects the evolution of Man was the opening of an entirely new chapter in the history of the universe. In no respect was it more so than in the genesis of the altruistic emotions. For when natural selection, through the lengthening of childhood, had secured a determinate development for this class of human feelings, it had at last originated a power which could thrive only through the elimination of strife. And the later history of mankind, during the past thirty centuries, has been characterized by the gradual eliminating of strife, though the process has gone on with the extreme slowness that marks all the work of evolution. It is only at the present day that, by surveying human history from the widest possible outlook, and with the aid of the habits of thought which the study of evolution fosters, we are enabled distinctly to observe this tendency. As this is the most wonderful of all the phases of that stupendous revolution in nature which was inaugurated in the Creation of Man, it deserves especial attention here; and we shall find it leading us quite directly to our conclusion. From the Origin of Man, when thoroughly comprehended in its general outlines, we shall at length be able to catch some glimpses of his Destiny.

XI.

Universal Warfare of Primeval Men.

IN speaking of the higher altruistic feelings as being antagonistic to the continuance of warfare, I did not mean to imply that warfare can ever be directly put down by our horror of cruelty or our moral disapproval of strife. The actual process is much more indirect and complex than this. In respect of belligerency the earliest men were doubtless no better than brutes. They were simply the most crafty and formidable among brutes. To get food was the prime necessity of life, and as long as food was obtainable only by hunting and fishing, or otherwise seizing upon edible objects already in existence, chronic and universal quarrel was inevitable. The conditions of the struggle for existence were not yet

visibly changed from what they had been
from the outset in the animal world.
That struggle meant everlasting slaughter,
and the fiercest races of fighters would be
just the ones to survive and perpetuate
their kind.   Those most successful primitive men, from whom civilized peoples are
descended, must have excelled in treach-
ery and cruelty, as in quickness of wit and
strength of will.   That moral sense which
makes it seem wicked to steal and murder
was scarcely more developed in them than
in tigers or wolves.   But to all this there
was one exception.   The family supplied
motives for peaceful coöperation.[12]   Within the family limits fidelity and forbearance had their uses, for events could not
have been long in showing that the most
coherent families would prevail over their
less coherent rivals.   Observation of the
most savage races agrees with the comparative study of the institutions of civilized
peoples, in proving that the only bond of
political union recognized among primitive

men, or conceivable by them, was the physical fact of blood-relationship. Illustrations of this are found in plenty far within the historic period. The very township, which under one name or another has formed the unit of political society among all civilized peoples, was originally the stockaded dwelling-place of a clan which traced its blood to a common ancestor. In such a condition of things the nearest approach ever made to peace was a state of armed truce ; and while the simple rules of morality were recognized, they were only regarded as binding within the limits of the clan. There was no recognition of the wickedness of robbery and murder in general.

This state of things, as above hinted, could not come to an end as long as men obtained food by seizing upon edible objects already in existence. The supply of fish, game, or fruit being strictly limited, men must ordinarily fight under penalty of starvation. If we could put a moral interpretation upon events which antedated morality as we understand it, we should say it was their duty to fight; and the reverence accorded to the chieftain who murdered most successfully in behalf of his clansmen was well deserved. It is worthy of note that, in isolated parts of the earth where the natural supply of food is abundant, as in sundry tropical islands of the Pacific Ocean, men have ceased from warfare and become gentle and docile without rising above the intellectual level of savagery. Compared with other savages, they are like the chimpanzee as contrasted with the gorilla. Such exceptional instances well illustrate the general truth that, so long as the method of obtaining food was the same as that employed by brute animals, men must continue to fight like dogs over a bone.

XII.

First checked by the Beginnings of Industrial Civilization.

BUT presently man's superior intelligence came into play in such wise that other and better methods of getting food were devised. When in intervals of peace men learned to rear flocks and herds, and to till the ground, and when they had further learned to exchange with one another the products of their labour, a new step, of most profound significance, was taken. Tribes which had once learned how to do these things were not long in overcoming their neighbours, and flourishing at their expense, for agriculture allows a vastly greater population to live upon a given area, and in many ways it favours social compactness. An immense series of social changes was now begun. Whereas the only conceivable bond of political combination had heretofore been blood-relationship, a new basis was now furnished by territorial contiguity and by community of occupation. The supply of food was no longer strictly limited, for it could be indefinitely increased by peaceful industry; and moreover, in the free exchange of the products of labour, it ceased to be true that one man's interest was opposed to another's. Men did not at once recognize this fact, and indeed it has not yet become universally recognized, so long have men persisted in interpreting the conditions of industrial life in accordance with the immemorial traditions of the time when the means of subsistence were strictly limited, so that one man's success meant another's starvation. Our robber tariffs — miscalled " protective " — are survivals of the barbarous mode of thinking which fitted the ages before industrial civilization began. But although the pacific implications of free exchange were very slowly recognized, it is not the less true that the beginnings of agriculture and commerce marked the beginnings of the greatest social revolution in the whole career of mankind. Henceforth the conditions for the maintenance of physical life became different from what they had been throughout the past history of the animal world. It was no longer necessary for men to quarrel for their food like dogs over a bone ; for they could now obtain it far more effectively by applying their intelligence to the task of utilizing the forces of inanimate nature ; and the due execution of such a task was in no wise assisted by wrath and contention, but from the outset was rather hindered by such things.

Such were the beginnings of industrial civilization. Out of its exigencies, continually increasing in complexity, have proceeded, directly or indirectly, the arts and sciences which have given to modern life so much of its interest and value. But more important still has been the work of industrial civilization in the ethical field. By furnishing a wider basis for political union than mere blood-relationship, it greatly extended the area within which moral obligations were recognized as binding. At first confined to the clan, the idea of duty came at length to extend throughout a state in which many clans were combined and fused, and as it thus increased in generality and abstractness, the idea became immeasurably strengthened and ennobled. At last, with the rise of empires, in which many states were brought together in pacific industrial relations, the recognized sphere of moral obligation became enlarged until it comprehended all mankind.

XIII.

Methods of Political Development, and Elimination of Warfare.

THIS rise of empires, this coalescence of small groups of men into larger and larger political aggregates, has been the chief work of civilization, when looked at on its political side.[13]   Like all the work of evolution, this process has gone on irregularly and intermittently, and its ultimate tendency has only gradually become apparent.   This process of coalescence has from the outset been brought about by the needs of industrial civilization, and the chief obstacle which it has had to encounter has been the universal hostility and warfare bequeathed from primeval times.   The history of mankind has been largely made up of fighting, but in the careers of the most

progressive races this fighting has been
far from meaningless, like the battles of
kites and crows. In the stream of history
which, beginning on the shores of the
Mediterranean Sea, has widened until in
our day it covers both sides of the At-
lantic and is fast extending over the re-
motest parts of the earth, — in this main
stream of history the warfare which has
gone on has had a clearly discernible purpose and meaning. Broadly considered,
this warfare has been chiefly the struggle
of the higher industrial civilization in de-
fending itself against the attacks of neighbours who had not advanced beyond that
early stage of humanity in which warfare
was chronic and normal. During the historic period, the wars of Europe have been
either contests between the industrial and
the predatory types of society, or contests
incident upon the imperfect formation of
large political aggregates. There have
been three ways in which great political
bodies have arisen. The earliest and low-

est method was that of *conquest without incorporation.* A single powerful tribe conquered and annexed its neighbours without admitting them to a share in the government. It appropriated their military strength, robbed them of most of the fruits of their labour, and thus virtually enslaved them. Such was the origin of the great despotic empires of Oriental type. Such states degenerate rapidly in military strength. Their slavish populations, accustomed to be starved and beaten or massacred by the tax-gatherer, become unable to fight, so that great armies of them will flee before a handful of freemen, as in the case of the ancient Persians and the modern Egyptians. To strike down the executive head of such an assemblage of enslaved tribes is to effect the conquest or the dissolution of the whole mass, and hence the history of Eastern peoples has been characterized by sudden and gigantic revolutions.

The second method of forming great

political bodies was that of *conquest with incorporation.* The conquering tribe, while annexing its neighbours, gradually admitted them to a share in the government. In this way arose the Roman empire, the largest, the most stable, and in its best days the most pacific political aggregate the world had as yet seen. Throughout the best part of Europe, its conquests succeeded in transforming the ancient predatory type of society into the modern industrial type. It effectually broke up the primeval clan-system, with its narrow ethical ideas, and arrived at the broad conception of rights and duties coextensive with Humanity. But in the method upon which Rome proceeded there was an essential element of weakness. The simple device of representation, by which political power is equally retained in all parts of the community while its exercise is delegated to a central body, was entirely unknown to the Romans. Partly for this reason, and partly because of the terrible military pressure to which the frontier was perpetually exposed, the Roman government became a despotism which gradually took on many of the vices of the Oriental type. The political weakness which resulted from this allowed Europe to be overrun by peoples organized in clans and tribes, and for some time there was a partial retrogression toward the disorder characteristic of primitive ages. The retrogression was but partial and temporary, however; the exposed frontier has been steadily pushed eastward into the heart of Asia; the industrial type of society is no longer menaced by the predatory type; the primeval clan-system has entirely disappeared as a social force; and warfare, once ubiquitous and chronic, has become local and occasional.

The third and highest method of forming great political bodies is that of *federation*. The element of fighting was essential in the two lower methods, but in this it is not essential. Here there is no conquest, but a voluntary union of small political groups into a great political group. Each little group preserves its local independence intact, while forming part of an indissoluble whole. Obviously this method of political union requires both high intelligence and high ethical development. In early times it was impracticable. It was first attempted, with brilliant though ephemeral success, by the Greeks, but it failed for want of the device of representation. In later times it was put into operation, with permanent success, on a small scale by the Swiss, and on a great scale by our forefathers in England. The coalescence of shires into the kingdom of England, effected as it was by means of a representative assembly, and accompanied by the general retention of local self-government, afforded a distinct precedent for such a gigantic federal union as men of English race have since constructed in America. The principle of federation was there, though not the name.

And here we hit upon the fundamental
contrast between the history of England
and that of France. The method by which
the modern French nation has been built
up has been the Roman method of conquest with incorporation. As the ruler of
Paris gradually overcame his vassals, one
after another, by warfare or diplomacy, he
annexed their counties to his royal domain, and governed them by lieutenants
sent from Paris. Self-government was thus
crushed out in France, while it was pre-
served in England. And just as Rome
achieved its unprecedented dominion by
adopting a political method more effective
than any that had been hitherto employed,
so England, employing for the first time
a still higher and more effective method,
has come to play a part in the world compared with which even the part played by
Rome seems insignificant. The test of
the relative strength of the English and
Roman methods came when England and
France contended for the possession of

North America. The people which pre-
served its self-government could send forth
self-supporting colonies ; the people which
had lost the very tradition of self-government could not. Hence the dominion of
the sea, with that of all the outlying parts
of the earth, fell into the hands of men of
English race ; and hence the federative
method of political union — the method
which contains every element of permanence, and which is pacific in its very conception — is already assuming a sway
which is unquestionably destined to become universal.

Bearing all this in mind, we cannot fail
to recognize the truth of the statement
that the great wars of the historic period
have been either contests between the industrial and the predatory types of society
or contests incident upon the imperfect
formation of great political aggregates.
Throughout the turmoil of the historic
period — which on a superficial view seems
such a chaos — we see certain definite

tendencies at work ; the tendency toward
the formation of larger and larger political
aggregates, and toward the more perfect
maintenance of local self-government and
individual freedom among the parts of the
aggregate. This two-sided process began
with the beginnings of industrial civilization ; it has aided the progress of industry
and been aided by it ; and the result has
been to diminish the quantity of warfare,
and to lessen the number of points at
which it touches the ordinary course of
civilized life. With the further continuance of this process, but one ultimate result is possible. It must go on until warfare becomes obsolete. The nineteenth
century, which has witnessed an unprecedented development of industrial civilization, with its attendant arts and sciences,
has also witnessed an unprecedented diminution in the strength of the primeval
spirit of militancy. It is not that we have
got rid of great wars, but that the relative
proportion of human strength which has

been employed in warfare has been re-
markably less than in any previous age.
In our own history, of the two really great
wars which have permeated our whole
social existence, — the Revolutionary War
and the War of Secession, — the first was
fought in behalf of the pacific principle
of equal representation ; the second was
fought in behalf of the pacific principle
of federalism. In each case, the victory
helped to hasten the day when warfare
shall become unnecessary. In the few
great wars of Europe since the overthrow
of Napoleon, we may see the same principle at work. In almost every case the
result has been to strengthen the pacific
tendencies of modern society Whereas
warfare was once dominant over the face of
the earth, and came home in all its horrid
details to everybody's door, and threatened
the very existence of industrial civilization ; it has now become narrowly confined
in time and space, it no longer comes
home to everybody's door, and, in so far

as it is still tolerated, for want of a better method of settling grave international questions, it has become quite ancillary to the paramount needs of industrial civilization. When we can see so much as this lying before us on the pages of history, we cannot fail to see that the final extinction of warfare is only a question of time. Sooner or later it must come to an end, and the pacific principle of federalism, whereby questions between states are settled, like questions between individuals, by due process of law, must reign supreme over all the earth.

XIV.

End of the Working of Natural Selection upon Man. Throwing off the Brute-Inheritance.

S regards the significance of Man's position in the universe, this gradual elimination of strife is a fact of utterly unparalleled grandeur. Words cannot do justice to such a fact. It means that the wholesale destruction of life, which has heretofore characterized evolution ever since life began, and through which the higher forms of organic existence have been produced, must presently come to an end in the case of the chief of God's creatures. It means that the universal struggle for existence, having succeeded in bringing forth that consummate product of creative energy, the Human Soul, has done its work and will presently cease. In the lower regions of

organic life it must go on, but as a deter-
mining factor in the highest work of evolution it will disappear.

The action of natural selection upon
Man has long since been essentially diminished through the operation of social
conditions. For in all grades of civilization above the lowest, "there are so
many kinds of superiorities which severally enable men to survive, notwithstand-
ing accompanying inferiorities, that natural
selection cannot by itself rectify any particular unfitness." In a race of inferior
animals any maladjustment is quickly re-
moved by natural selection, because, owing
to the universal slaughter, the highest
completeness of life possible to a given
grade of organization is required for the
mere maintenance of life. But under the
conditions surrounding human development it is otherwise.[14] There is a wide
interval between the highest and lowest
degrees of completeness of living that
are compatible with maintenance of life.

7

Hence the wicked flourish. Vice is but slowly eliminated, because mankind has so many other qualities, beside the bad ones, which enable it to subsist and achieve progress in spite of them, that natural selection — which always works through death — cannot come into play. The improvement of civilized man goes on mainly through processes of direct adaptation. The principle in accordance with which the gloved hand of the dandy becomes white and soft while the hand of the labouring man grows brown and tough is the main principle at work in the improvement of Humanity. Our intellectual faculties, our passions and prejudices, our tastes and habits, become strengthened by use and weakened by disuse, just as the blacksmith's arm grows strong and the horse turned out to pasture becomes unfit for work. This law of use and disuse has been of immense importance throughout the whole evolution of organic life. With Man it has come to be paramount.

If now we contrast the civilized man intellectually and morally with the savage, we find that, along with his vast increase of cerebral surface, he has an immensely greater power of representing in imagination objects and relations not present to the senses. This is the fundamental intellectual difference between civilized men and savages.[15] The power of imagination, or ideal representation, underlies the whole of science and art, and it is closely connected with the ability to work hard and submit to present discomfort for the sake of a distant reward. It is also closely connected with the development of the sympathetic feelings. The better we can imagine objects and relations not present to sense, the more readily we can sympathize with other people. Half the cruelty in the world is the direct result of stupid incapacity to put one's self in the other man's place. So closely inter-related are our intellectual and moral natures that the development of sympathy is very considerably determined by increasing width and variety of experience. From the simplest form of sympathy, such as the painful thrill felt on seeing some one in a dangerous position, up to the elaborate complication of altruistic feelings involved in the notion of abstract justice, the development is very largely a development of the representative faculty. The very same causes, therefore, deeply grounded in the nature of industrial civilization, which have developed science and art, have also had a distinct tendency to encourage the growth of the sympathetic emotions.

But, as already observed, these emotions are still too feebly developed, even in the highest races of men. We have made more progress in intelligence than in kindness. For thousands of generations, and until very recent times, one of the chief occupations of men has been to plunder, bruise, and kill one another. The selfish and ugly passions which are primordial — which have the incalculable strength of inheritance from the time when animal consciousness began — have had but little opportunity to grow weak from disuse. The tender and unselfish feelings, which are a later product of evolution, have too seldom been allowed to grow strong from exercise. And the whims and prejudices of the primeval militant barbarism are slow in dying out from the midst of peaceful industrial civilization. The coarser forms of cruelty are disappearing, and the butchery of men has greatly diminished. But most people apply to industrial pursuits a notion of antagonism derived from ages of warfare, and seek in all manner of ways to cheat or overreach one another. And as in more barbarous times the hero was he who had slain his tens of thousands, so now the man who has made wealth by overreaching his neighbours is not uncommonly spoken of in terms which imply approval. Though gentlemen, moreover, no longer assail one an-

other with knives and clubs, they still in-
flict wounds with cruel words and sneers.
Though the free - thinker is no longer
chained to a stake and burned, people still
tell lies about him, and do their best to
starve him by hurting his reputation. The
virtues of forbearance and self-control are
still in a very rudimentary state, and of
mutual helpfulness there is far too little
among men.

Nevertheless in all these respects some
improvement has been made, along with
the diminution of warfare, and by the
time warfare has not merely ceased from
the earth but has come to be the dimly
remembered phantom of a remote past,
the development of the sympathetic side
of human nature will doubtless become
prodigious. The manifestation of selfish
and hateful feelings will be more and more
sternly repressed by public opinion, and
such feelings will become weakened by
disuse, while the sympathetic feelings will
increase in strength as the sphere for

their exercise is enlarged. And thus at length we see what human progress means. It means throwing off the brute-inheritance, — gradually throwing it off through ages of struggle that are by and by to make struggle needless. Man is slowly passing from a primitive social state in which he was little better than a brute, toward an ultimate social state in which his character shall have become so transformed that nothing of the brute can be detected in it. The ape and the tiger in human nature will become extinct. Theology has had much to say about original sin. This original sin is neither more nor less than the brute-inheritance which every man carries with him, and the process of evolution is an advance toward true salvation. Fresh value is thus added to human life. The modern prophet, employing the methods of science, may again proclaim that the kingdom of heaven is at hand. Work ye, therefore, early and late, to prepare its coming.

XV.

The Message of Christianity.

NOW what is this message of the modern prophet but pure Christianity? — not the mass of theological doctrine ingeniously piled up by Justin Martyr and Tertullian and Clement and Athanasius and Augustine, but the real and essential Christianity which came, fraught with good tidings to men, from the very lips of Jesus and Paul! When did St. Paul's conception of the two men within him that warred against each other, the appetites of our brute nature and the God-given yearning for a higher life, — when did this grand conception ever have so much significance as now? When have we ever before held such a clew to the meaning of Christ in the Sermon on the Mount? "Blessed are the meek, for they

shall inherit the earth." In the cruel strife
of centuries has it not often seemed as if
the earth were to be rather the prize of the
hardest heart and the strongest fist? To
many men these words of Christ have been
as foolishness and as a stumbling-block,
and the ethics of the Sermon on the Mount
have been openly derided as too good for
this world. In that wonderful picture of
modern life which is the greatest work of
one of the great seers of our time, Victor
Hugo gives a concrete illustration of the
working of Christ's methods. In the saint-
like career of Bishop Myriel, and in the
transformation which his example works in
the character of the hardened outlaw Jean
Valjean, we have a most powerful com-
mentary on the Sermon on the Mount.
By some critics who could express their
views freely about "Les Misérables" while
hesitating to impugn directly the authority
of the New Testament, Monseigneur Bienvenu was unsparingly ridiculed as a man of
impossible goodness, and as a milksop and

fool withal. But I think Victor Hugo understood the capabilities of human nature, and its real dignity, much better than these scoffers. In a low stage of civilization Monseigneur Bienvenu would have had small chance of reaching middle life. Christ himself, we remember, was crucified between two thieves. It is none the less true that when once the degree of civilization is such as to allow this highest type of character, distinguished by its meekness and kindness, to take root and thrive, its methods are incomparable in their potency. The Master knew full well that the time was not yet ripe, — that he brought not peace, but a sword. But he preached nevertheless that gospel of great joy which is by and by to be realized by toiling Humanity, and he announced ethical principles fit for the time that is coming. The great originality of his teaching, and the feature that has chiefly given it power in the world, lay in the distinctness with which he conceived a state of society from which every vestige of strife, and the modes of behaviour adapted to ages of strife, shall be utterly and forever swept away. Through misery that has seemed unendurable and turmoil that has seemed endless, men have thought on that gracious life and its sublime ideal, and have taken comfort in the sweetly solemn message of peace on earth and good will to men.

I believe that the promise with which I started has now been amply redeemed. I believe it has been fully shown that so far from degrading Humanity, or putting it on a level with the animal world in general, the doctrine of evolution shows us distinctly for the first time how the creation and the perfecting of Man is the goal toward which Nature's work has been tending from the first. We can now see clearly that our new knowledge enlarges tenfold the significance of human life, and makes it seem more than ever the chief object of Divine care, the consummate fruition of that creative energy which is manifested throughout the knowable universe.

XVI.

The Question as to a Future Life.

UPON the question whether Humanity is, after all, to cast in its lot with the grass that withers and the beasts that perish, the whole foregoing argument has a bearing that is by no means remote or far-fetched. It is not likely that we shall ever succeed in making the immortality of the soul a matter of scientific demonstration, for we lack the requisite data. It must ever remain an affair of religion rather than of science. In other words, it must remain one of that class of questions upon which I may not expect to convince my neighbour, while at the same time I may entertain a reasonable conviction of my own upon the subject.[16] In the domain of cerebral physiology the question might be debated forever without a result. The only thing which cerebral physiology tells us, when studied with the aid of molecular physics, is against the materialist, so far as it goes. It tells us that, during the present life, although thought and feeling are always manifested in connection with a peculiar form of matter, yet by no possibility can thought and feeling be in any sense the products of matter. Nothing could be more grossly unscientific than the famous remark of Cabanis, that the brain secretes thought as the liver secretes bile. It is not even correct to say that thought goes on in the brain. What goes on in the brain is an amazingly complex series of molecular movements, with which thought and feeling are in some unknown way correlated, not as effects or as causes, but as concomitants. So much is clear, but cerebral physiology says nothing about another life. Indeed, why should it? The last place in the world to which I should go for information about a state of things in which thought and feeling can exist in the absence of a cerebrum would be cerebral physiology!

The materialistic assumption that there is no such state of things, and that the life of the soul accordingly ends with the life of the body, is perhaps the most colossal instance of baseless assumption that is known to the history of philosophy. No evidence for it can be alleged beyond the familiar fact that during the present life we know Soul only in its association with Body, and therefore cannot discover disembodied soul without dying ourselves. This fact must always prevent us from obtaining direct evidence for the belief in the soul's survival. But a negative presumption is not created by the absence of proof in cases where, in the nature of things, proof is inaccessible.[17] With his illegitimate hypothesis of annihilation, the materialist transgresses the bounds of experience quite as widely as the poet who sings of the New Jerusalem with its river of life and its streets of gold. Scientifically speaking, there is not a particle of evidence for either view.

But when we desist from the futile attempt to introduce scientific demonstration into a region which confessedly transcends human experience, and when we consider the question upon broad grounds of moral probability, I have no doubt that men will continue in the future, as in the past, to cherish the faith in a life beyond the grave. In past times the disbelief in the soul's immortality has always accompanied that kind of philosophy which, under whatever name, has regarded Humanity as merely a local incident in an endless and aimless series of cosmical changes. As a general rule, people who have come to take such a view of the position of Man in the universe have ceased to believe in a future life. On the other hand, he who regards Man as the consummate fruition of creative energy, and the chief object of Divine care, is almost irresistibly driven to the belief that the soul's career is not completed with the present life upon the earth. Difficulties on theory he will naturally expect to meet in many quarters ; but these will not weaken his faith, especially when he remembers that upon the alternative view the difficulties are at least as great. We live in a world of mystery, at all events, and there is not a problem in the simplest and most exact departments of science which does not speedily lead us to a transcendental problem that we can neither solve nor elude. A broad common-sense argument has often to be called in, where keen-edged metaphysical analysis has confessed itself baffled.

Now we have here seen that the doctrine of evolution does not allow us to take the atheistic view of the position of Man. It is true that modern astronomy shows us giant balls of vapour condensing into fiery suns, cooling down into planets fit for the support of life, and at last growing cold and rigid in death, like the moon. And there are indications of a time when systems of dead planets shall fall in upon their central ember that was once a sun, and the whole lifeless mass, thus regaining heat, shall expand into a nebulous cloud like that with which we started, that the work of condensation and evolution may begin over again. These Titanic events must doubtless seem to our limited vision like an endless and aimless series of cosmical changes. They disclose no signs of purpose, or even of dramatic tendency;[18] they seem like the weary work of Sisyphos. But on the face of our own planet, where alone we are able to survey the process of evolution in its higher and more complex details, we do find distinct indications of a dramatic tendency, though doubtless not of purpose in the limited human sense. The Darwinian theory, properly understood, replaces as much teleology[19] as it destroys. From the first dawning of life we see all things working together toward one mighty goal, the

8

evolution of the most exalted spiritual qualities which characterize Humanity. The
body is cast aside and returns to the dust
of which it was made. The earth, so
marvellously wrought to man's uses, will
also be cast aside. The day is to come,
no doubt, when the heavens shall vanish
as a scroll, and the elements be melted
with fervent heat. So small is the value
which Nature sets upon the perishable
forms of matter! The question, then, is
reduced to this: are Man's highest spiritual qualities, into the production of which
all this creative energy has gone, to disappear with the rest? Has all this work
been done for nothing? Is it all ephemeral, all a bubble that bursts, a vision
that fades? Are we to regard the Crea-
tor's work as like that of a child, who
builds houses out of blocks, just for the
pleasure of knocking them down? For
aught that science can tell us, it may be
so, but I can see no good reason for be-
lieving any such thing. On such a view

the riddle of the universe becomes a riddle without a meaning. Why, then, are we any more called upon to throw away our belief in the permanence of the spiritual element in Man than we are called upon to throw away our belief in the constancy of Nature? When questioned as to the ground of our irresistible belief that like causes must always be followed by like effects, Mr. Mill's answer was that it is the result of an induction coextensive with the whole of our experience; Mr. Spencer's answer was that it is a postulate which we make in every act of experience;[20] but the authors of the "Unseen Universe," slightly varying the form of statement, called it a supreme act of faith, — the expression of a trust in God, that He will not "put us to permanent intellectual confusion." Now the more thoroughly we comprehend that process of evolution by which things have come to be what they are, the more we are likely to feel that to deny the everlasting persistence of the spiritual element in Man is to rob the whole process of its meaning. It goes far toward putting us to permanent intellectual confusion, and I do not see that any one has as yet alleged, or is ever likely to allege, a sufficient reason for our accepting so dire an alternative.

For my own part, therefore, I believe in the immortality of the soul, not in the sense in which I accept the demonstrable truths of science, but as a supreme act of faith in the reasonableness of God's work. Such a belief, relating to regions quite inaccessible to experience, cannot of course be clothed in terms of definite and tangible meaning. For the experience which alone can give us such terms we must await that solemn day which is to overtake us all. The belief can be most quickly defined by its negation, as the refusal to believe that this world is all. The materialist holds that when you have described the whole universe of phenomena of which we can become cognizant under the conditions of the present life, then the whole story is told. It seems to me, on the contrary, that the whole story is not thus told. I feel the omnipresence of mystery in such wise as to make it far easier for me to adopt the view of Euripides, that what we call death may be but the dawning of true knowledge and of true life. The greatest philosopher of modern times, the master and teacher of all who shall study the process of evolution for many a day to come, holds that the conscious soul is not the product of a collocation of material particles, but is in the deepest sense a divine effluence. According to Mr. Spencer, the divine energy which is manifested throughout the knowable universe is the same energy that wells up in us as consciousness. Speaking for myself, I can see no insuperable difficulty in the notion that at some period in the evolution of Humanity this divine spark may have acquired sufficient concentration and steadiness to survive the wreck of material forms and endure forever. Such a crowning wonder seems to me no more than the fit climax to a creative work that has been ineffably beautiful and marvellous in all its myriad stages.

Only on some such view can the reasonableness of the universe, which still remains far above our finite power of comprehension, maintain its ground. There are some minds inaccessible to the class of considerations here alleged, and perhaps there always will be. But on such grounds, if on no other, the faith in immortality is likely to be shared by all who look upon the genesis of the highest spiritual qualities in Man as the goal of Nature's creative work. This view has survived the Copernican revolution in science, and it has survived the Darwinian revolution. Nay, if the foregoing exposition be sound, it is Darwinism which has placed Humanity upon a higher pinnacle than ever. The future is lighted for us with the radiant colours of hope. Strife and sorrow shall disappear. Peace and love shall reign supreme. The dream of poets, the lesson of priest and prophet, the inspiration of the great musician, is confirmed in the light of modern knowledge ; and as we gird ourselves up for the work of life, we may look forward to the time when in the truest sense the kingdoms of this world shall become the kingdom of Christ, and he shall reign for ever and ever, king of kings and lord of lords.

REFERENCES.

C. P., Outlines of Cosmic Philosophy, 1874; U. W., The Unseen World, 1876; D., Darwinism and Other Essays, 1879; E. E., Excursions of an Evolutionist, 1884.

1. C. P. ii. 432–451.
2. C. P. ii. 89–91.
3. C. P. ii. 318–321; D. 45.
4. U. W. 40–42; D. 65–74; E. E. 278–282, 327-336.
5. C. P. ii. 154–159.
6. C. P. ii. 133–135.
7. D. 45–48; E. E. 306–319.
8. C. P. ii. 310.
9. E. E. 109–146.
10. C. P. ii. 284–323.
11. C. P. ii. 342–346, 358–363.
12. C. P. ii. 202–208.
13. C. P. ii. 213–224.
14. C. P. ii. 334.
15. C. P. ii. 312–315.
16. U. W. 54; E. E. 289–291.

17. U. W. 47–50; D. 75.

18. D. 96–102.

19. C. P. ii. 406.

20. C. P. i. 45–71, 286; ii. 162; U. W. 6; D. 87–95.

For EU product safety concerns, contact us at Calle de José Abascal, 56–1°,
28003 Madrid, Spain or eugpsr@cambridge.org.